This is not a fairy tale – it's real!

Pictures by Bedřich Fritta
To Tommy for his Third Birthday
in Terezín, 22 January 1944

Text by Ivan Klíma

Translated by Stephen Hattersley

ŽIDOVSKÉ
MUZEUM
PRAHA

Jewish Museum in Prague 2000

I dedicate this book to my wife Věra, who is now with my parents in peace,
and to my children David, Daniel, Ronny and Michal
and to all children throughout the world.

Words emerge, words disappear, they come and go. The words that have been used to describe the fate of those who disappeared for ever can fill the whole universe. Still, my father Bedřich and mother Hansi remain where they had to end, without blame. Wherever I go I show this book of my father's which is full of life, hope and love and whose strength prevails. There will always be people, both young and old, who will look at these pictures that were done in a place of no return, pictures which gave my father the strength to complete what for him was the most important thing, that is to create a vision of the world where there is sun, color and light, a book full of imagination and love for his son. Every time I think of my parents, whose faces I find it hard to picture, I feel as if part of me has been amputated. On the other hand, I can see them as I want to - full of light and love - and so I hand this book on to my children and grandchildren.

Tommy Fritta-Haas

I had to move several times while I was in Terezín, where I was forced to stay for as long as the ghetto was in existence. From 1942 I was staying in the former Riding Barracks where to this day, large sculpted horses' heads rise above the gates. The Nazis, who renamed everything, called it Magdeburg. We lived in a small room directly above the rear gate. Next door, in just as small a room, lived three painters with their families - Mr. Fritt, Mr. Haas and Mr. Ungar. I greatly admired them, for at the time I imagined I would also become a painter, once the war was over. I often watched them as they were portraying life in the courtyard outside their window. Mr. Haas once asked me to sit for him and he drew my portrait in ink. I don't know whether the drawing survived, probably not. Mr. Fritta drew a picture of my brother on his birthday, either his fifth or sixth, as well as a similar book to the one you are now reading, except there were fewer pictures and they weren't in color. But it did include nursery rhymes which the young poet Mirko Tůma had written specially for my brother. There were pictures of animals, such as a cat, a dog and a pig which had the following rhyme:
A pig eats with glee
All that he can see
Even enough for three
This rhyme has stayed in my memory, but the pictures have unfortunately disappeared for ever, as have the other rhymes.

What is worse is that the artists also disappeared. We knew that people were sent away in transports, but the artists were taken away separately, just with their wives and children. I can still remember the moment they left. I can even remember little Tommy crying.

I only found out that he had survived when, many years after the war, I received these pictures and was asked to base a story on them. I met Tommy again some twenty years later. It was a long time since our childhood, but when I was writing this story, based on his pictures, about the boy who didn't become a number, I thought a lot about those dark distant days, when we were forced to live in two adjacent rooms, waiting for the war to end and dreaming of a different, freer world.

Ivan Klíma

In 1941-1945 the garrison town of Terezín became the largest concentration camp in Bohemia and Moravia. 140,000 Jews passed through Terezín, mostly from the Protectorate of Bohemia and Moravia, Germany, Austria and Holland. Around 88,000 prisoners were deported to the extermination camps in the east, while almost 34,000 died in the ghetto through hunger, exhaustion and illness. 17,000 Terezín prisoners survived. By some miracle, four-year-old Thomas (the son of the painter, Bedřich Fritta, and his wife Hanse) was rescued from the overcrowded cells in the Lesser Fortress.

The Prague artist Bedřich Fritta (b. Fritz Taussig, 19 September 1906 near Frýdlant, North Bohemia - d. 8 November 1944 in Auschwitz) came to Terezín in one of the first transports on 4 December 1942. He worked in the art room of the ghetto's Technical Office and on evenings would secretly draw pictures depicting life in the ghetto - transports arriving and departing, the daily suffering and death of the elderly, the accumulation of coffins in the mortuary. One day, some of his drawings were found during a search in the ghetto. As a result, Bedřich Fritta, Otto Ungar, Leo Haas and Ferdinand Bloch were arrested for alleged "propaganda of terror", questioned and, on 17 July 1944, sent with their families to the SS prison in the Lesser Fortress. Most of them did not survive. Seriously ill, Bedřich Fritta was deported with Leo Haas on 26 October to Auschwitz and died of blood poisoning shortly after arrival. His wife died of typhoid fever on 13 February 1945 in the Lesser Fortress. The four-year-old Thomas survived thanks to the care he received from Erna Haasová, with whom he shared a cell until the end of the war.

Leo Haas passed through Auschwitz, Sachsenhausen, Mauthausen and Ebensee and was the only one from the group of artists who survived. After the war, Erna and Leo Haas adopted little Thomas Fritta and then settled in Prague. Erna Haasová died in 1955.

Thomas Fritta-Haas grew up in Prague and emigrated to Israel after the Soviet Occupation of 1968. He left for West Germany shortly before the Yom Kippur War of 1973. A librarian by profession, he has four children, and lives alternately in Prague and Mannheim.

Thomas Fritta has kept the picture book which his father drew for him in Terezín for his third birthday (22 January 1944) in memory of his father. His father hid the book inside a wall shortly before he was arrested. After liberation, Leo Haas recovered it, along with other pictures, which he handed over to Thomas. The pictures show a world that existed on the other side of the Terezín walls, a world of the future, which Bedřich Fritta knew was not within his reach.

Arno Pařík

As I look at the pictures in this book, which as yet is without words, apart from those sketched underneath by the painter many years ago, I wonder just what I should tell you - for I am to add the words and sentences.

Fairy tales are usually told to children. These generally start with the words: "Once upon a time," but such stories are only make-believe.

To Tommy!

TOMÍČKOVI !

As I look at the pictures, I remember what happened. I knew the artist who painted these pictures at the time he painted them. That was during the war, when I was about the same age as you are now. The painter lived in a room next to mine, which I shared with my parents, my brother and various other people. That room was within the barracks - we lived there even though we weren't soldiers.

When my brother was five years old, the artist drew him a picture book in which were lots of animals and verses. The book disappeared and all I remember of it is the smiling piglet, under which were the following lines:

A pig eats with glee
All that he can see
Even enough for three

I could tell you something about the time when I was the same age as you are now, about how we lived in a barracks even though we weren't soldiers, about the painter and the small boy for whom these pictures were painted, about the evil war. It may sound like a fairy tale to you, but I know it all actually happened, even though a long, long time ago, when I was as small as you are now.

To Tommy on his third birthday in Terezín – 22 January 1944

Tomíčkovi

K JEHO 3. NAROZENINÁM !
V TEREZÍNĚ - 22. I. 1944 !

In those days, the country bordering mine was governed by a cruel and crazy ruler. We'll call him the ruler of darkness because his officials and guards wore black uniforms and had the sign of the sinister skull and cross-bones on their caps. These were similar to the markings on the wings of a hawk-moth, although the hawk-moth, unlike the guards of darkness, is an innocent creature that doesn't harm anyone.

The crazy ruler declared himself infallible and omnipotent as God. All who were willing to revere him were accepted as his armed henchmen, even if they were thieves, cut-throats or any other criminals. He then began to persecute those who were just, honest and wise, those who wanted no war, those who believed in God rather than in him, the ruler of darkness, those who had curly hair or large noses, and those whose parents had curly hair or large noses, as well as many other people. First of all, he persecuted those in his own country and after that in the countries conquered by his army.

Tommy's sleepy

TOMMY HAJÁ!

My country, like many others, was occupied by the troops of the ruler of darkness. With them came the officials and guards of darkness in black uniforms and with the skull and cross-bones on their caps. They immediately started to draw up lists of people who they found just, honest and wise, those who believed in God instead of the ruler of darkness, those who had curly hair, those who wanted no war, those who had large noses, those whose parents had curly hair or large noses, as well as many others. Our painter, his wife and their small boy, who was but an infant, all found themselves on such a list, as did my parents, my brother and I, who was then the same age as you are today.

Pee pee ...

PIPEPÉÉ.....

The people on these lists could have filled the houses and streets of a large city. Amongst them were doctors and blacksmiths, barbers and zoo keepers, chauffeurs, lawyers, scholars and teachers, violinists, miners, gardeners and owners of scooter shops, bookstore assistants, engineers, scholars and chemists, barons, farmers, astronomers, engine-drivers and, as you already know, painters, their wives and their children, as well as those who would be born to them.

A good boy – no spanky spanky

HODNÉÉJ-

BARI - BARI - NÉÉ

The officials and guards of darkness with the skull and cross-bones on their caps then bound these lists into a thick volume which they sent to the ruler of darkness. He was just about to attack a neighboring ruler's large empire, as he was preparing for a big war, the biggest war ever to be experienced by people and to be witnessed by countries, the sun and the moon, a war in which he would defeat all other rulers, both good and evil, and conquer their countries, conquer the whole world.

Tommy foooooood!

TOMMY PAPÚÚÚ !

The officials of darkness bowed down and cried "Long live our great, our greatest ruler," whereupon they handed him the volume.

The ruler of darkness took the volume into his hands and opened it. As he was preparing for the big war, however, he had no time for reading, so he immediately closed it. "Put them all to death!" he shouted and, without even waiting for his officials to respond, he went to his chambers. Here maps were spread across huge tables and around them crowded the generals who were helping him prepare for the big war.

Tommy more! More!

The officials of darkness were left with the volume: "Put them all to death!" they repeated to themselves. That meant doctors, blacksmiths and barbers, zoo keepers, chauffeurs, lawyers, scholars and teachers, violinists, miners, gardeners and owners of scooter shops, bookstore assistants and engineers, chemists, farmers, astronomers, engine-drivers and painters, their wives and their children. But what if they don't comply? After all, nobody wants to be put to death. The officials of darkness were afraid that people would run away, hide in the forests and mountains, and then perhaps revolt and put them, the officials of darkness, to death. That is why they decided to trick them. They sent out a decree ordering that none of those whose names were in the thick volume may leave their town or go into the forest, and also that they will come to no harm.

Jester!

KOMEDIANTE!

Those affected - and you know just how many there were - were very frightened. They considered revolting, but how could they win when they had no weapons? The soldiers of darkness are capable of anything, while we have always gone about our work in an honest way. It's bad, they admitted, that they are not allowed to leave their home town or go into the forest, but at least in their town there are plenty of nice parks and street-lined avenues, and they can swim in the river or go to cafés, restaurants and candy stores. They can see shows at the theater and films at the cinema, listen to music at concerts or on the radio, and visit friends. Even like that, they'll be able to live. The main thing is that nothing worse will happen to them.

Tommy pees here!

TOMMY LULU TÁM!

The officials of darkness were satisfied and immediately issued another decree. This time, all those not allowed to leave the town and go into the forest were also forbidden from entering public gardens and swimming in the river. Those affected became even more frightened but consoled themselves: although it's bad that they are not allowed to leave their home town, go into the forest or park or swim in the river, they had no choice in the matter, as they couldn't fight against the guards of darkness who are capable of anything. At least they can walk through gardens, go to cafés, restaurants and candy stores, see shows at the theater and films at the cinema, listen to music at concerts or on the radio, and visit friends. Even like that they'll be able to live. The main thing is that nothing worse is happening.

Tommy draws

TOMMY MALUJE

The officials of darkness were satisfied and immediately issued another decree. As you rightly guess, they now forbade all those poor people, who were no longer allowed to leave their town, to go into the forest or park or to swim in the river, from walking through gardens, seeing shows at the theater or films at the cinema, going to cafés, restaurants, listening to music at concerts or on the radio, and visiting friends. They also forbade them from working in their workplaces, making telephone calls and traveling in cars and trolley-buses. They were not allowed in the front carriages of trams and very soon they were not even allowed in the rear, which meant that they had to walk. They were also forbidden from going to shops where other people went and from buying clothes and shoes, good meat and fruit, and then flowers and onions, chocolate, honey, cheese and sweets.

Mommy!! My pacifier!!

DUDLE!! AJTÁÁÁ!!

They were then ordered to stitch a special sign on their breast pocket, so that they could be recognized by everybody. One by one they were then summoned and told: Long ago you ceased to be doctors, blacksmiths, barbers, zoo keepers, chauffeurs or lawyers. You are nothing, you are not human beings, for you don't even go to the forest or the park, you don't swim in the river, you aren't interested in the theater or the cinema, and you don't listen to music. You are now nothing but numbers, numbers on a list, with no need for names.

A person who has a name, reasoned the officials of darkness, has his place amongst people - he has ancestors after whom he was named, he has his place in the world and his name plate on the door. But he who doesn't even have a name is of no interest to anybody. Nobody will remember him or cry for him if he disappears from the world.

Big Tommy, little Tommy

VELKÝ   MALÝ

TOMMY

And so, each of those registered in the thick volume was allotted a number, and the officials of darkness shouted out: If you are nothing but numbers, what are you doing amongst other people. They were then ordered to pack their essentials in a case, to put their allotted number on the lid and to hang the same number around their neck. The numbered people were then taken away to an old fortress and once there, moved into the army barracks, even though they weren't soldiers.

When the people wanted to leave the barracks and the fortress into which they had been taken, they realized they couldn't, as they were actually in prison.

It was in the barracks, from whose windows one could see the red-brick fortifications and the gates closely guarded by armed guards, that we met – the painter, his small boy and myself.

Snow!

We each had our own number. The small boy, as you may have noticed from the picture, had the number AAL 710. He was one and a half years old when they brought him into the barracks. Like his father the painter, his mother, myself, my father, in fact just like everybody in this fortress town, he was to be put to death.

Soup – tea – coffee warmmmm!

POJÍKA - TÁJ - KAFE
HÓÓÓKÝ !

This is where you probably expect a brave knight and his followers to appear, the legendary hero shouting at the ruler of darkness and his villainous henchmen: "Stop this right now!" But no such person appears - after all, this is not a fairy tale but a story from the war that actually happened. No knight appears. Only somewhere in the distance, the soldiers of the ruler of darkness are fighting the soldiers of other rulers, but that is so far away that no one in the barracks, even during the deep silence of midnight, can hear their steps or the shots from their guns. All that could be heard were the steps of the officials of darkness as they moved amongst the helpless prisoners, picking out those to be put to death the next day.

Tommy sweeps

TOMMY UMETÁ !

Would you like to know what a small boy does in such a town that is a prison, or what he does in the huge barracks where a great many strangers are packed together and where the officials of darkness can appear at any time to drag them away to their lairs and put them to death? Is he unhappy? Does he cry wherever he goes? Does he tremble with fear?

Tommy owwww!

TOMMY BEBÉ'É'É' !

Well, even in such a place as this, a small boy does what boys all over the world do. He gets up in the morning, his mom gets a little water and washes his eyes so that they are even bluer than before, then brushes his hair which is the color of ripe ears of corn, and helps him get dressed and ties his shoelaces. As the small boy is hungry, his mom gives him some bread and jam with a drink of substitute coffee. The bread smells of mold, the jam of rotten sugar-beet. The small boy has never seen butter, eggs, cheese, ham or tomatoes. He has never eaten chocolate, nuts or roasted cereals. He hasn't even ever tasted cocoa, whipped cream or fruit juice. But what the small boy eats and drinks is not that important for him - he just wants to finish his breakfast and play in the barracks yard with the other boys. What games can they play in the barracks yard? Well, they play with a ball, chase each other or play hopscotch with the girls. When it snows in the winter they make snowmen. The small boy has never seen a forest or a park, flowers growing in the meadow, the river as it flows, or ships and steamboats sailing by. He hasn't even seen a single dog or a cow, a sheep, a lamb, a rabbit or a hen, let alone a turtle, a swan or a flamingo.

By the table!!

When it rains, the boy stays in his room which he shares with many other people and plays with his doll which his parents put in his suitcase as they were leaving their home town. He also plays with a brush, a coal shovel and a poker. Or he takes his father's prayer book and pretends to pray.

For lunch, his mom may give him potatoes and mustard, with or without sauerkraut. The boy has never eaten good meat, fish, salad, cucumber, turnip, carrots, corn or beans. He's never even tasted a single cherry, let alone a peach, an orange or a banana.

Chocopoopoo

MAMELAKAKAKAKA

In the late afternoon, the boy takes a little nap. His mom kisses him on his forehead and wishes him sweet dreams. But what can he dream about if he knows nothing of the world, if he hasn't even seen a forest or a park, flowers growing in the meadow, the river as it flows, ships and steamboats sailing by, or if he hasn't even seen a dog, a cow, a sheep, a lamb or a hen, let alone a turtle, a swan or a flamingo - if he has never seen anything of beauty?

Clown!

ŠAŠKU!

Has he really not seen anything of beauty? Hasn't he seen the sun and the moon, the stars in the sky, snowflakes or the patterns frost makes on the window? Can't he see from his window the beautiful lime trees which are clothed in leaves from springtime and have the sweet scent of honey in early summer? Don't the swallows nest on the walls of the barracks? Doesn't he hear the singing of the finches and thrushes each morning? And what about the people around him? It's true that some are sad and care-worn, but others smile at him, hold his hand and take him for walks around the barracks yard or even along the street between the barracks. And then there's his father, the painter - I'd almost forgotten about him. He mostly paints sad pictures depicting the suffering of the people whom the officials of darkness intend to change into numbers and whom the guards intend to put to death.

A parcel – a parcel!!

BALÍK – BALÍK !!

He draws people pulling heavy carts such as horses pull, as well as sick old men and women, and people waiting in long lines for food. But he realizes that his small boy must also know something about life outside the gates, if he is to remain human as those outside and not become a number as the officials of darkness intend. This is why, when he returns each morning, he paints pictures for his small boy. He paints him a large mirror so that he will know what a mirror actually is. He paints him a parcel full of goodies that he has never tasted before. He paints him flowers, butterflies, fish, a car and gingerbread. He paints him an engineer, a detective, a boxer, a business man and a general. He also paints him the sun and the moon for him to see, even if they are hiding in the sky behind clouds.

Tommy too!

And then there's his mom who, like all moms, tells him stories. As long as people tell each other stories, as long as they are able to imagine things that are hidden from them, as long as they care how things happen, they can never become numbers.

What stories does his mom tell him? Well, she tells him fairy tales and talks about the world that is outside the fortress and about his dad's pictures. She tells him about the mirror, the moon and the sun.

What can she tell him about the sun?

She tells him that the sun gives out light and heat. More in summer and less in winter.

Why is it warmer in summer? asks the boy.

In summer the earth tilts more towards the sun, and the days are longer which means it's warmer.

Can you pull the sun a bit closer in winter so it's warm in winter as well?

No, you can't pull the sun closer as it's very big and heavy. Besides that, there's nothing you could pull it with.

Couldn't you pull the sun closer with a very long rod?

No, the sun is too far away.

Couldn't you pull the sun closer with the longest rod in the world?

Tommy prays

TOMMY MODLÍ

No, the sun is too far away. Besides that, even if someone had such a long rod and reached the sun, he couldn't pull the sun as the rod would melt.

But a rod can't melt.

Even a rod would burn on the sun. Everything would burn on the sun.

Even a stove?

Yes, even a stove would melt on the sun.

Would a chimney melt on the sun?

Yes, even a chimney would melt on the sun.

If chimneys melt, what do they use for heating?

They don't use anything because there are no people there.

If there were people on the sun, would they also melt?

Yes, even people would melt.

And what about birds?

Even birds would melt.

But don't birds ever use their wings to fly to the sun?

Mommy – daddy are cross!

Well, it may happen that a bird thinks it can fly as far as the sun. The other birds try to talk him out of it, as some of them have already tried to fly to the sun but became too exhausted to carry on. Nevertheless, the bird takes no heed and decides to take off the following Sunday.

On Sunday the bird gets up early and cleans his wings with great care. He has a drink from the stream and a hearty breakfast, for he knows from the other birds who have tried to get to the sun that it is a long and difficult journey. He says good-bye to all the other birds, picks up in his little claws a bit of food for a snack, something for lunch and even for supper, for he knows that it will be a really long journey, and then takes off. He flies with his beak pointed straight up at the sun and he flaps his wings, but only slowly, for he knows that he wouldn't get anywhere if he got tired too soon.

Uncle

So, he's in the air and actually rising upwards. First of all, he sees the forest where he took off from, then the houses and church spires and the river flowing around the forest. He can still hear the other birds in the forest, the call of the cuckoo, the whistle of a train and the ringing of church bells. But as he rises higher and higher, the sounds become more faint, the forest and houses disappear and the river is but a glittering thread. The bird then sees clouds lying just ahead of him like white mountains and snow-covered hills, and as he flies over them it's already midday. He can no longer see the ground or hear anything. All he sees are the mountain-like clouds beneath him. He flies higher and higher, and above him he now only sees the sun and the sky, which is becoming less blue and gradually merging into blackness.

Dumplings, pudding, potatoes, meat, water, cream

KEDLÍKEK

PUDINK

BAMBUNKY MAKO

ODA

KÉM

The bird starts to feel a little tired, so he stops flapping his wings for a while and just glides at that great height. He has a snack and then rises once more. The clouds beneath him are no longer visible, and the sky is empty and cold. The bird continues to fly towards the sun. By now he is tired, but he still rises, reaching for the sun. Come the evening, the bird finishes his last bit of food and continues to rise. He can't see the sun, just stars. He feels like sleeping but knows he must go on, for the sun is far away. So he rises higher and higher. All night long he flaps his wings until he feels he really can't go on. In his mind he pictures a forest and a branch on which he could rest for just a short while. In the morning, when the sun rises once again, the bird is completely alone and can see nothing but the sky and the rising sun. All of a sudden he notices something terrible - the sun is just as far away as before. Although he had been flying all day and all night without a moment's rest, the sun was no nearer. It's then that the bird realizes that even if he were to fly another day and night and then many more days and nights, he still wouldn't reach the sun, since it is too far away.

Cow – moo, chirpchirp, bowwow, baah!

KRÁVIKA — MÚ   PÍP

HAF HAF   BÉÉÉ !

Is the sun really so far away? asks the small boy.

Yes, the sun is so far away.

And what does the bird do now?

The bird flies back to the forest and tells all the other birds about his journey and advises them not to fly to the sun as they will only tire themselves out and won't get there anyway. Some birds listen, but others say they'll have a go anyway.

Cup, eye, glasses, spoon, bowl

HYNEKEK

OKO

BÝLE

ÍKA

TAJÍK

By the time his mom finishes the story, the small boy has already closed his eyes and is sinking into a dream. He sees a beautiful bird with broad fiery wings. This is a phoenix, which he has never seen before, either flying over the lake or perching in the zoo. Now he sees it high in the sky in this wonderful dream which makes him smile in his sleep.

Auto – toot toot

AUTO-TUTÚ

Another time, his mom tells him of the river.

The small boy has never seen a river. He hasn't even seen a brook or a stream. Such things are not to be seen in the fortress town. He only knows the puddles left by the rain and the water that comes out of the water-pipes. People wait in long lines with pots and pans for this water. He also knows the water in the tin wash-basin where he washes and plays with his blue paper boat. His dad the painter made it for him. But the boy cannot imagine where a river comes from, with all that continually flowing water.

Water flows out of the ground like a spring, explains his mom.

And how did the water get in the ground?

The water fell onto the ground out of the clouds.

And where do clouds come from?

Clouds come out of the sea. The sea is bigger than the biggest river. It's so vast that nobody can see where it ends. Even birds that fly over the sea have to fly whole days and nights before they can cross it.

And what does the sea do with so much water?

White, blue, red, green – light

Nothing. Water is just there. It is silent or it roars, it makes waves that spill over. Some water is deep, dark and cold. Other water tosses against the lonesome rock called the Black Cliff, and basks in the sun, thinking about how up to now it has seen nothing but water around it. It has never even seen a mountain or an animal or a human being - just fish or seagulls, stormy petrels and other sea birds. So the water asks the birds if there is a way of getting away from the sea and glimpsing something else other than water, but the birds don't know. From one wave the water eventually learns that if it doesn't protect itself from the sun, a miracle occurs and the water is able to travel.

My mommy, daddy Bedudu

MOJE MAMINKA

TÁTA BEDUDU !

And how does that happen? asks the water from the Black Cliff, but the wave has already flowed away into the distance. All the water knows is that it should lie down in the sun and not hide for a moment in the shade of the Black Cliff.

So one particularly hot day, the water says good-bye to all its friends, the fish, sea-horses and sea-urchins, and then lies on the surface and waits. The sun beats down on the water making it shimmer and glisten until it starts to tremble. And all of a sudden, the water has no idea what is happening to it - it is lighter than ever before and starts to rise, higher and higher. Soon it is high above the sea and the first thing it sees underneath is the immense glistening surface. So much water. Farewell sisters, it cries to the waves. It can see them shimmering in the sun and their white crests tossing over the azure surface. It then notices that many of its sisters are floating alongside.

The moon sleeps – blanket – pillow

MĚSÍČEK HAJÁ – DEKOU – POLKAT

Where are you floating to? asks the water. We don't know, they reply. We were lying in the sun when we suddenly felt dizzy. We were so light that we started to rise. And now we're floating.

And because they feel anxious and sad, so high above the sea, they press together for comfort thus forming a cloud which the wind moves on even further.

What happens to this cloud?

The cloud floats above the sea in the direction of land. Meanwhile, on the land it is so hot that in some regions all the water supply has dried up. Not only the puddles, but the brooks, streams, rivers and even the deep wells in which there had always been water. All that is alive - grass, bushes, trees, animals and people - is dying of thirst. People, dogs, cows, horses, sheep and lambs, all look up to the sky which is also hot, so hot that it is almost white. The people notice that all the birds have flown away. They then get down on their knees and start to pray: if it doesn't rain today, we'll perish, oh God, they beg, we have nothing to drink. Even if we had something to drink, even if we found a little water, our fields will dry up, not a single potato will grow, and we'll starve to death.

The sun is on the potty

SLUNÍČKO
DĚLA A-A

Meanwhile, the water from the Black Cliff is clinging to its companions, floating faster and faster until it glimpses something it has never seen before. It is still in the distance but getting closer. It is something dark, immense and steep, a mountain on the coast, almost bare but for a few pine trees on the top. The water is getting closer and is afraid that it will crash into the stone mountain or break against the pine trunks. However, the cloud swings over the mountain and the water floats on. Full of curiosity, the water looks down and first of all sees houses and smoke coming out of the black jaws of chimneys. It then sees a chimney-sweep walking along a roof, but takes him for a beetle. The water floats above the church spires and above the railway tracks, along which is hurtling a train carrying people wet with perspiration and weary from the heat. One of them looks out the window: just look at those clouds, he says, how they shimmer.

Bim, bim, bim – our train is on the way

BIM, BIM, BIM
NÁŠ VLAK JEDE...

By now the water is a little tired, yet it looks down at the strange shapes of rocks and at the forests. It sees the shimmering and glistening rivers. Then it notices that the rivers have disappeared, leaving behind dry river beds. As dawn breaks, the water sees a parched landscape covered in dust. It sees the people run out of their houses and look up at the cloud. It notices that even the animals - dogs, cows, horses, sheep and lambs - all raise their weary heads and look up at the cloud. It observes the people wringing their hands and imagines that it almost hears their voices.

We're off on our travels – somewhere cold or somewhere warm?

JDEM NA CESTY —

KDE JE IMA NEBO HOKÓ ?

The water floats on but feels pity for the parched earth and for the people wringing their hands. It has a strange feeling of languor and heaviness as if, all of a sudden, it can no longer maintain such a height. Sisters, the water cries, I feel dizzy, I'm going to fall! It holds on with all its might to the cloud, yet is not able to take its eyes away from the people down below, crying and raising their hands. The water feels it can no longer hold on and, broken into a thousand drops, falls to the ground. Farewell sisters, it cries, but then notices they are all descending together.

Here – or there?

NEBO SEM — ČI TAM?

What will happen to me? asks the water.

The people run out of their houses and catch the drops of water with their open mouths. The dogs, cows, horses, sheep and lambs run to the dried up river, down which now run the first trickles, and drink the Black Cliff water which for them means life.

The small boy now knows what the sea looks like and how rivers emerge, even though he has never seen them and even though, at most, all he can hear when darkness falls on the fortress town is the rumbling of the weir outside the ramparts, where he is not allowed.

Or would you rather travel like this?

NEBO CHCEŠ CESTOVAT TAK?

So, although the boy may live in a fortress town surrounded by guards of darkness who intend to change him into a number and then put him to death, there are times when he is completely fine and content, like children anywhere else in the world.

Well, you must be eager to know what becomes of the small boy, his mom and dad, and all the people in the barracks, as well as the guards of darkness. Does the brave knight finally appear with his army?

Or would you prefer to go by plane?

NEBO RADŠÍ LETADLEM?

But have you forgotten again that this is not a fairy tale.

It's true that somewhere in the far off distance, the armies of other rulers are fighting the pillaging armies of the ruler of darkness, but this is so far away that it couldn't be seen by even the sharpest eye. Meanwhile, the guards and officials of darkness are running around the town, selecting from the people they brought there for execution. Whoever is instructed must leave with them, never to be seen again. When will they notice the small boy, his dad and mom? When will they notice me, who lives in the next room?

Or "only" as far as the river?

It would be good to hide or to run away from this terrible fortress town. But how could you escape from here when there is an armed guard at the gate.

And then his mom and dad get an idea. They disguise the small boy as a railwayman so that no one will be able to recognize him, not even the guards of darkness. Then the small boy gets on the train which supplies the town with wood, coal, food and people. At the last moment, his mom passes him a large suitcase. Later on, we'll find out just what is inside, but he knows he cannot open it yet as time is short and his life is at stake. The train whistles, lets out a plume of steam and sets off.

We wonder who your bride will be?

As soon as the train leaves the town, the small railwayman walks on tiptoe and puffs out his chest so that he will look bigger and broader and so that he can see the country-side which he has never seen before - the forests and parks, the flowers blooming in the meadows, the rivers flowing, the ships and steam-boats sailing by. He also wants to see the dogs, cows and horses, sheep, lambs and rabbits, hens, turtles, swans and fla-mingos. He knows that he has a long journey ahead of him. He has to get beyond the borders of the empire governed by the ruler of darkness and his armed henchmen. He has to get as far as the land of long winters where the Eskimos live, or the land of eter-nal heat where the black-skinned races live, or somewhere even further where the Chinamen or Sioux or Cherokee Indians live. But will he get there at all? What if some-body realizes that it is him, the small boy disguised as a railwayman escaping from the barracks, the fortress town and the prison of the ruler of darkness? Wouldn't it be better if he traveled in a different way. Maybe he should mount a giant turtle disguised as a Turk or board a plane in which he could get away more quickly.

This is not a fairy tale – it's real!

TO NENÍ POHÁDKA - TO JE PRAVDA!

Meanwhile, the officials of darkness are checking their numbers. They count the prisoners in the barracks, compare the number with their lists, and suddenly realize that one prisoner is missing. They inform the guards of darkness who in turn inform their supreme commander who immediately calls the alarm. He summons all his guards, soldiers and policemen, firemen, railwaymen and sailors, airmen, hunters and hotel doormen, as well as a pack of police dogs. All shout, run, search, sneak about, make inquiries and spy. Then one of the railway men remembers seeing on the train that left the fortress town an extremely small blue-eyed railwayman in a completely new uniform, under whose cap was flapping fine hair the color of ripe ears of corn.

That was him, cry the officials of darkness rushing to telephones and telegraphs to cable the order: Immediately search all trains and hold the small railwayman. He has a new uniform, blue eyes and hair the color of ripe ears of corn.

This too is not a fairy tale!

I TO NENÍ — POHÁDRA!

The guards of darkness rush around all the stations in search of the small railway man.

On seeing them, the small boy is so scared that he trembles all over. What will happen to him if the guards of darkness recognize him? He won't be able to get anywhere. It will mean the end of his journey with no chance of returning to his mom and dad. At the last moment, however, he remembers his suitcase, opens it up, and what does he see? The case is full of clothes, all kinds of disguises. On top lies a great detective's out-fit together with wig, pipe and checked cap. The small boy only just manages to get into the disguise when the guards of darkness enter his compartment. They greet the great detective and inquire as to whether he has seen a small railwayman in a brand new uniform, with blue eyes and hair the color of ripe ears of corn.

And when we get somewhere – somewhere in the world

A AŽ NĚKAM PŘÍJDEM

— NĚKAM NA SVĚTĚ —

He got off the train, says the small detective in the deepest voice he could command. It was ten stops down the line, you blockheads!

As soon as they hear this, and without a word of thanks, the guards of darkness jump off the train. They immediately telephone their chief to inform him that they haven't found the small railwayman but that they have at least come across an important lead. They work out which is the tenth stop back and they send a great number of soldiers and policemen, firemen, railwaymen and sailors, airmen, hunters and hotel doormen, as well as two packs of police dogs. They all begin searching houses, attics and cellars, sheds, summer houses and shacks, goat sheds, dog kennels and canary cages. They shine their torches through the sewers, pull apart hay stacks and even search the bags of passers-by, but the small blue-eyed railwayman is nowhere to be seen.

Then I'll buy music for you, too

TAK MUJIKU TI TAKÉ KOUPÍM

Who was it that actually put you onto this important lead? asks the supreme commander.

It was the great detective himself, reply the guards.

Just how big was this great detective?

Well he was rather small, admit the guards.

What color were his eyes?

We didn't see them, they were hidden under his peaked cap.

What color was his hair? screams the commander.

His hair was also hidden under his cap, whisper the guards of darkness.

And what would you like to be? An engineer?

You stupid blockheads, screams the supreme commander. Don't you know who this small great detective was?

By now the guards of darkness of course know and are already scrambling in all directions. They are joined in their search for the small great detective by a great number of soldiers and policemen, firemen, railwaymen and sailors, airmen, hunters and hotel doormen, as well as a pack of police dogs.

They comb the inns, pubs and taverns, churches, cathedrals and chapels, shops, toilets and bathrooms, look inside children's satchels, tip out soil from flower-pots and sweets from paper cones, and question whoever they meet about the small great detective.

They also want to question the famous boxer who is fighting this very moment in the ring, but nobody dares, for the boxer is looking at them in a threatening manner with a raised right hand on which is a huge glove. Who would dare disturb him when he is in the middle of a fight? Anyway, he can't have seen anybody while he was skipping around between the ropes, the guards say to themselves as they walk off.

You stupid blockheads! You numskulls! Their commander screams at them, just how big was this famous boxer?

Actually, he was rather small, admit the guards.

And what about the color of his eyes? And what about his hair? roars the supreme commander. He then decides to put himself at the head of his uniformed men and lead the search. He gets in a car and speeds off to the boxing ring.

Or a famous detective?

NEB VELKÝM DETEKTIVEM?

Is that small famous boxer still here?

The boxer has already left. Walking past the commander, probably to his car, is a general with helmet and crest and covered in medals, stars, crosses and decorations, his saber rattling against his spurs.

The supreme commander stands to attention, raises his arm in salute and cries: Long live the ruler of darkness and his generals!

The general casually nods and walks off.

The commander of darkness looks around the boxing ring in vain when suddenly it dawns on him: just how big was that general? Wasn't he a bit small? And where was his car?

The supreme commander immediately instructs his guards: Everyone, follow me, find the small general!

Things now look pretty bad for the small general. After all, he hasn't got a car, he can't run away as his sword gets in the way and he can't put on any more disguises as there aren't any left.

At this moment, the small boy wakes up. He blinks his eyes, not knowing where he is and then realizes that he is in the barracks and hasn't escaped anywhere. Should he be glad? Can he be sure that nobody is really after him, that a guard of darkness won't come into the room and take him away.

Well, you probably want to know if the boy escapes, if he manages to break free from the barracks and the fortress town.

Or a boxer?

NEBO BOXEREM?

But I have already said that this is not a fairy tale. A fairy tale can be illustrated for the boy by his dad or told by his mom. Just as his dad painted a railwayman, a detective, a boxer and a general, he also paints a garden full of flowers, butterflies and bees with the small boy in the middle, bathing in a pool. He also paints a kind greengrocer woman selling tulips and ox-eye daisies, plums, strawberries, cauliflower and apples as well as other goodies, under which he writes: This is not a fairy tale! Even if it does seem just like a fairy tale to the small boy. His dad also draws eggs and apples, pears and grapes, sausages, cream, cake, chocolate and sweets. None of this is a fairy tale, he says, this is peace.

What is peace? asks the small boy who until now has known nothing but war.

His dad then draws a dove, the sun and the Statue of Liberty. He draws good food and drink.

Is all this peace?

Yes. But peace is much more, says his dad. Peace cannot be described in drawings or in words. Peace is the opposite of war, but neither can war be described in drawings or in words. War and peace can only be experienced.

So the boy does not know what peace is. All he knows is war, the barracks, food in a tin bowl, and the guards of darkness who guard the gates and walk around night and day selecting those who they intend to put to death. The boy only suspects that peace is something that everybody looks forward to and waits for with longing.

Or a painter?

A NEB MALÍŘEM ?

Grown-ups know many things in which they can find pleasure before going to sleep. They can think of life outside the gates of the dark town, their homes, towns, the mountains, theater shows, concerts, people they like. And they know so many strange and special words whose meanings are as yet unknown to the boy. What is he to think about? What is he to look forward to?

Sometimes, when he's falling asleep, he imagines he sees bright lights. These are just ordinary light bulbs, but with his eyes half closed, the lights start to flicker like butterflies, which is something he likes. He thinks that this must be what peace is like. Another time he sees the water that he knows from his dad's pictures and his mom's tales. He sees a big river which rolls and ripples along to the sea. It smells like rain and is like a huge mirror in which sail the moon, trees, rocks and stars, fish winding their way among them. The small boy also goes there on a blue paper boat, saying to himself: this is peace. He also pictures toys, such as a drum and stick and a violin, as well as bizarre trees on which they say grow large, sweet and fragrant fruits and nuts. Trees you can drill holes in and drink milk from.

That is peace.

This is how the small boy looks forward to peace.

No doubt you would like to know what became of the painter, his wife and small boy. You would like to hear how they were rescued from the clutches of the guards of darkness.

Just not a businessman, please!

But this is not a fairy tale. War is still raging, occasionally a plane drones in the sky, and somewhere in the distance can be heard thunderous clashes, the sound of houses crashing down. The sounds of the screams and cries of people, however, do not reach the town.

I remember how one day the guards of darkness and their cruel assistants appeared in our corridor. Petrified, we waited to see what would happen. They came closer and closer and then stormed into the room where lived the painter, his wife and small boy, as well as other painters and their wives and children, and took them all away, never to be seen again in the fortress town.

My story is now coming to an end.

The armies of the ruler of darkness eventually weaken and flee from the countries they have conquered and pillaged. The ruler of darkness himself crawls into a deep concrete bunker where he screams that he will never surrender, that he must conquer the whole world and put to death all his enemies, all just, honest and wise people, all those who are against war and all those who believe in God instead of in him, but you already know what he was ranting about. Now, however, fewer and fewer people listen, even though his words are relayed through loudspeakers in all the towns still held by his armies. Such towns are becoming fewer and fewer, as the soldiers of the ruler of darkness throw down their weapons and flee.

And not a general!

A TAKÉ NE GENERÁLEM!

The ruler of darkness now starts to realize that he will never conquer the world or put to death all those people he wanted to put to death. He knows instead that he will be put before a court and condemned for everything he has done. So the ruler of darkness orders that a revolver be brought to him. For a moment he trembles with fear, and then he shoots himself.

On hearing this, the soldiers of darkness start to take off their uniforms, throw them aside and then bury them in the ground. This marks the end of the war which my story was about. My story should also end here. But you would like to know what became of the small boy, his mom and dad the painter who were all dragged away from the fortress town by the guards of darkness.

The small boy was taken to an even more confined and dark prison and locked in a cold cell without windows where he trembled with fear and became hungry. But as you know, the ruler of darkness was dead, and so now the cell door is flung open and the small boy is told he is free.

What is it to be free? asks the small boy.

They tell him that he can come out of the dark cell. He can go into the yard or even further, to the forest, the river, along the bridge, down the lane and through the meadow, where he can turn somersaults, run, skip, play with his ball and then go back to the town where he once lived, where he was born. He can go to the park, walk through the gardens and go into a candy store. He can go wherever he wants.

And what about my mom and dad? asks the small boy.

All of this and twice as many wishes for your next birthday – daddy Bedudu

A JEŠTĚ JEDNOU TOLIK TI PŘEJE
NA PŘÍŠTÍ SVÁTEČEK — BEDUDU

But nobody knows where his mom and dad are. The small boy is put in a big car with a red cross on it and led out of the prison. He'll soon be five years old, but he has never before seen a real forest or park or flowers blooming in the meadow. So now he looks around and sees everything. He sees the river flowing, a boat sailing by, cattle, horses and sheep grazing and dogs barking. He sees houses and people he doesn't know but who wave at him.

And then it occurs to him that something incredible has happened. Peace has come.

And what about his mom and dad?

Well, I wish this was a fairy tale and I could tell you that they all met up safe and sound and happily embraced. But this is a story of what happened during the war, which I lived through when I was the same age as you are now, and so all I can say is that the small boy never saw his mom and dad again.

Several of his dad's pictures survived, some of which you will see in this book. Among them is a picture of his mom who told such wonderful stories that, even behind the walls of the fortress town that was ruled by the guards of darkness, the small boy could enjoy moments of happiness, the kind that children all over the world enjoy.

And both were survived by the small boy who didn't become a number.

And for 1944 I wish you health (raspberry juice, California fruit), etc! Your Bedudu

A PŘEJI TI PRO 1944

ZDRAVÍČKO, ATD !

TVŮJ Bednin

This book is the first in a long line of books that I intend to draw for you!

TATO KNIHA JEST

PRVNÍ

V DLOUHÉ ŘADĚ KNIH,

KTERÉ MÁM V ÚMYSLU

TI NAMALOVAT!

THIS IS NOT A FAIRY TALE – IT'S REAL!

To Tommy, for his Third Birthday in Terezín, 22 January 1944

Illustrations © Tommy Fritta-Haas

Text © Ivan Klíma

Translation © Stephen Hattersley

© Jewish Museum in Prague 2000

First English edition

ISBN: 80-85608-35-9

Printed by Label, Kutná Hora